The Houseplant Almanac

Christine Walkden

Lochar Publishing . Moffat . Scotland

To all those who help me when I need it most. You know who you are.

Published by Lochar Publishing Ltd, Moffat, Scotland, DG10 9ED.

A catalogue record for this book is available from the British Library

ISBN 1-874027- 02-1
Typeset in Optima 8.5pt on 10pt by The Image Works, New Lanark, and printed by Cambus Litho.

Contents

Acknowedgements
4

Introduction
5

Flowering Plants for Well-Lit Positions
7 – 45

Foliage Plants for Well-Lit Positions
47 – 59

Flowering Plants for Partial or
Semi-Shaded Positions
61 – 86

Foliage Plants for
Semi-Shaded Positions
87 – 113

Plants for Shaded Positions
115 – 132

Glossary of Common Terms

Index of Common Names

Index of Botanical Names

Acknowledgements

I would like to express my sincere thanks to George Brown and Lochar Publishing and their staff for making this book possible.

Hilary Course not only allowed me to use her word processor for this publication, but taught me how to use it in the process of my writing the book. Her patience, kindness and encouragement were all necessary and most gratefully received.

Two nurseries allowed me to photograph their plants. At the Dutch Nursery at Bell Bar, Hatfield, Herts, I thank the Hen family for great freedom and assistance. Thanks also to Rochfords at Crews Hill for pulling back the thermal screens when necessary.

Christine M. Walkden
October 1991

Introduction

Houseplants are becoming increasingly popular in today's homes, not only for their beauty but also because they are thought to act as air filters and to improve the atmosphere by absorbing unwanted gases.

However, I still find that most houseplants are killed through over-watering, under-watering or putting them in the wrong place.

This publication is intended to provide a succinct and simple guide, answering all the basic questions asked by the gardener, enabling him or her to maintain the plants in good condition over many years.

Feeding of most houseplants should take place throughout the growing season. This means from April through to late September. Once light levels start to decline in the autumn, the plants' growth naturally slows down, and their requirement for fertilizer stops. Feeding beyond September can result in very soft growth which is prone to pest and disease attack and the production of leaves at the expense of flowers.

For flowering plants feeding with a potash-rich fertilizer is ideal. This can either be bought as a potash-rich houseplant fertilizer or as a tomato fertilizer. Note the manufacturers' instructions for application rates and frequency unless otherwise stated in the text.

Houseplants can be grown by anyone, even the person who has never grown a plant before. If you happen to kill one or two on the path to success, do not be put off. The only real way to learn how to grow your plants is by growing them, using the tips in this book to help you gain the necessary experience.

May I wish you many happy hours caring for and enjoying some of the plants detailed in this guide.

Flowering Plants for Well-Lit Positions

Common names	Hot water plants, Cupid's bower.
Botanical name	*Achimenes* 'Rosy Red'.
Interesting facts	Name probably from the Greek, meaning not surviving the winter, being frost sensitive. Also thought to be named after King Hakhamash of Turkey.
Origin	Tropical areas of America and Mexico.
Position	Well-lit but away from direct sun in summer.
Temperature	Minimum winter temperature 55F.
Watering	Use tepid water to keep compost moist at all times during growing season. Once flowering stops allow to dry, cut off stems and store rhizomes in dry peat over winter.
Feeding	Every 2 weeks throughout growing season with potash-rich house plant fertilizer.
Humidity	Do not wet leaves. Stand pots on damp gravel tray and keep moist at all times.
Re-potting	Re-pot rhizomes into fresh compost in early spring.
Propagation	From rhizomes or stem cuttings taken in May.

Common name	African lilies.
Botanical name	*Agapanthus.*
Interesting facts	Name derived from Greek, *agape,* love and *anthos,* a flower.
Origin	South Africa.
Position	Full sun.
Temperature	Minimum winter temperature of 40–45F.
Watering	Maintain dampness in the compost throughout growing season. From November to early April give very little water.
Feeding	During growing season with potash-rich fertilizer.
Humidity	Misting is not necessary.
Re-potting	Not required until division takes place.
Propagation	Divide plant every 4–5 years.

Common name	Belladonna lily.
Botanical name	*Amaryllis belladonna.*
Interesting facts	Named after a shepherdess mentioned in Theocritus and Virgil, Greek and Latin poets.
Origin	South Africa.
Position	Full sun.
Temperature	Minimum winter temperature of 50F.
Watering	Start watering when growth begins. Allow compost surface to dry out between waterings.
Feeding	During growing season with potash-rich fertilizer.
Humidity	Mist leaves occasionally.
Re-potting	Every 3–5 years.
Propagation	Offsets at re-potting time.

Common name	Wax Begonia.
Botanical name	*Begonia semperflorens.*
Interesting facts	The specific name *semperflorens* means 'always flowering'.
Origin	Brazil.
Position	Bright light but not direct sunlight.
Temperature	Not less than 55F in winter.
Watering	Compost should be moist throughout growing season, but allow surface to dry out between waterings.
Feeding	Throughout growing season with potash-rich fertilizer.
Humidity	Mist leaves frequently, but never wet the flowers. Stand pots on gravel trays.
Re-potting	Normally thrown away after flowering as they are treated as annuals.
Propagation	From seed sown in spring.

Common name	Begonia.
Botanical name	*Begonia tuberhybrida.*
Interesting facts	Tuberous hybrids derived mainly from *B. boliviensis, B. pearcei* and *B. rosaeflora.*
Origin	Garden origin.
Position	Well-lit position away from direct sun.
Temperature	Minimum winter temperature 55F.
Watering	Water frequently when plant is in flower. Compost should not however be constantly soggy.
Feeding	Feed regularly throughout growing season with potash-rich fertilizer.
Humidity	Mist plants frequently and surround pots with damp compost or peat.
Re-potting	Normally tuber is thrown away after flowering, or dried off, stored over winter in peat and potted in spring.
Propagation	Pot tubers in spring.

Common name	Shrimp plant.
Botanical name	*Beloperone guttata.*
Interesting facts	*Beloperone* is derived from the Greek *belos,* an arrow and *perone,* a buckle – a reference to the way the anther lobes are connected.
Origin	Mexico.
Position	Well-lit, with some direct light.
Temperature	Minimum winter temperature 45F.
Watering	Water well throughout growing season but sparingly in winter.
Feeding	Throughout growing season with potash-rich fertilizer.
Humidity	Mist leaves occasionally.
Re-potting	Re-pot in spring if necessary.
Propagation	Stem cuttings.

Common name	Paper flower.
Botanical name	*Bougainvillea x buttiana* 'Brilliant'.
Interesting facts	Named after French navigator who sailed around the world in 1767-69, Louis Antoine de Bougainville.
Origin	A hybrid between *B. glabra* and *B. peruviana.*
Position	Full sun.
Temperature	Minimum winter temperature 45F.
Watering	Water well throughout growing season, keeping compost almost dry in winter.
Feeding	Throughout season with potash-rich fertilizer.
Humidity	Mist frequently if grown in heated room.
Re-potting	Only if essential in the spring.
Propagation	Stem cuttings in summer.

Common name	Bush violet.
Botanical name	*Browallia speciosa* 'Blue Troll'.
Interesting facts	The plant is thought to be named after J. Browallius, Bishop of Abo, Sweden, who was also a botanist.
Origin	Colombia.
Position	Bright light with some direct sun.
Temperature	Minimum winter temperature 50F.
Watering	Compost should be moist throughout growing season.
Feeding	Throughout season with potash-rich fertilizer.
Humidity	Mist leaves occasionally.
Re-potting	Normally grown as an annual and thrown away after flowering.
Propagation	Sow seeds in spring or summer.

Common names	The slipper flower, Pocket book plant.
Botanical name	*Calceolaria x herbeohybrida.*
Interesting facts	Named after F. Calceolari, 16th-century Italian botanist.
Origin	Garden hybrid.
Position	Bright, but away from direct light.
Temperature	Cool, between 50–60F.
Watering	Compost should be moist at all times.
Feeding	Throughout growing season with potash-rich fertilizer.
Humidity	Do not mist leaves or flowers, but stand pots on a pebble tray and keep moist.
Re-potting	Normally seed grown, pricked out into 3.5 inch pots, then into 5 inch pots.
Propagation	By seed in summer in a cool greenhouse for flowering the following year. Throw plants away after flowering.

Common name	Bottlebrush plant.
Botanical name	*Callistemon citrinus.*
Interesting facts	From the Greek *kallistos,* beautiful, and *stemon* ,a stamen. The beauty of the flower is the bright red stamens. The foliage is lemon-scented.
Origin	Australia and New Caledonia.
Position	Good well-lit position, but out of direct sunlight.
Temperature	Minimum winter temperature 45F.
Watering	Water well from spring until autumn, then keep on the dry side throughout the winter.
Feeding	From April–September with a potash-rich fertilizer.
Humidity	Misting is not necessary.
Re-potting	Re-pot when necessary in late April.
Propagation	Stem cuttings in the spring.

Common names	Italian bellflower, Star of Bethlehem, The Bell Flower.
Botanical name	*Campanula isophylla.*
Interesting facts	Name derived from the Latin for 'a little bell'.
Origin	North-west Italy.
Position	Well-lit spot, but avoid direct sun in summer.
Temperature	Minimum winter temperature of 45F.
Watering	Keep compost moist during the growing season, but reduce amount in winter months.
Feeding	Throughout growing season with potash-rich fertilizer.
Humidity	Occasionally mist the leaves.
Re-potting	Re-pot every spring.
Propagation	Stem cuttings in spring. Seed in the spring or division at re-potting.

Common names	Pot mum, Florist's chrysanthemum.
Botanical name	*Chrysanthemum morifolium.*
Interesting facts	Named after the Greek *chrysos*, gold, and *anthos*, a flower.
Origin	From China in 1764.
Position	Good bright light is necessary but plants should be shaded from midday sun.
Temperature	Cool, between 50–60F, especially when in flower to extend flowering.
Watering	Plants should be moist at all times.
Feeding	Throughout growing season with potash-rich fertilizer.
Humidity	Mist leaves occasionally.
Re-potting	Normally not necessary as plant is sold just before flowering.
Propagation	Due to cultural techniques employed by the professional to dwarf the plants, it is not easy for the amateur to produce good results.

Common names	Parrot's bill, Koka beak, Lobster claw, Glory pea.
Botanical name	*Clianthus puniceus 'Albus'.*
Interesting facts	Name derived from the Greek meaning 'Glory flower'.
Origin	New Zealand.
Position	Full sun.
Temperature	Minimum winter temperature 50F.
Watering	Water well from spring until autumn, letting the compost surface dry slightly between waterings. During winter water sparingly.
Feeding	Throughout growing season with balanced plant fertilizer.
Humidity	Mist leaves on warm days or stand on a gravel tray.
Re-potting	Re-pot when necessary in the spring.
Propagation	Sow seeds in the spring. Stem cuttings in the summer.

Common name	The Kaffir lily.
Botanical name	*Clivia miniata.*
Interesting facts	Named after a Duchess of Northumberland, Lady Charlotte Florentina Clive, who died in 1868.
Origin	Warm dry forests of South Africa.
Position	Bright light, but avoid direct sun in summer as it may scorch the leaves.
Temperature	Minimum winter temperature of 40–50F. This is necessary for the flower to form.
Watering	Water lightly from late autumn to early spring until the flower spike is 6 inches high, then water well ensuring that entire root ball is moist.
Feeding	Do not feed during winter months, thereafter use a house plant fertilizer rich in potash.
Humidity	Sponge leaves occasionally to remove dust and freshen plant.
Re-potting	After flowering, and only when roots have absolutely filled the pot.
Propagation	By division at time of re-potting.

Common name	Firecracker flower.
Botanical name	*Crossandra undulifolia (infundibuliformis).*
Interesting facts	Name derived from Greek, *krossus*, a fringe, and *aner*, male, referring to the fringed anthers. *Undulifolia* means wavy foliage.
Origin	India, Sri Lanka.
Position	Well-lit position but avoid direct light in summer.
Temperature	Minimum winter temperature of 55F.
Watering	During the growing season the compost should be moist all the time. Reduce the amount in winter.
Feeding	Throughout growing season with potash-rich fertilizer once a week.
Humidity	Stand pots on damp gravel tray and keep atmosphere moist.
Re-potting	Only re-pot if necessary in the spring before flowering.
Propagation	Stem cuttings in the summer or seed in the spring.

Common name	Crown of thorns.
Botanical name	*Euphorbia milii splendens.*
Interesting facts	The sap is poisonous so keep away from eyes and mouth. Named after Euphorbus, physician to Juba, King of Mauritania.
Origin	Madagascar. *E. milii* is said to be named after M. Millius, governor of the Isle of Bourbon.
Position	Well-lit but shade from direct sun in summer.
Temperature	Minimum winter temperature 55F.
Watering	Water moderately during growing season, letting surface of compost dry between waterings. Reduce frequency in the winter months.
Feeding	Every 2 weeks from April–September with a potash-rich fertilizer.
Humidity	Misting is not necessary.
Re-potting	Re-pot every second spring if necessary.
Propagation	Stem cuttings in June and July. Allow milky sap to dry before placing in compost.

Common name	Poinsettia.
Botanical name	*Euphorbia pulcherrima.*
Interesting facts	Introduced in 1834 and named in honour of the Mexican traveller and American Minister to Mexico, Joel Roberts Poinsett, who first found the plant in 1828.
Origin	Native of Mexico and tropical America.
Position	Maximum light is necessary during winter; sunny position during summer months but out of direct sun.
Temperature	Minimum winter temperature of 55–60F.
Watering	Water well during the flowering season so that the entire pot is wet.
Feeding	From July feed weekly with potash-rich houseplant fertilizer.
Humidity	Mist leaves frequently during the flowering season.
Re-potting	Not normally necessary as the plant is generally bought in flower and normally thrown away after flowering.
Propagation	Stem cuttings in early summer. Not widely practised by the home gardener.

Common name	Fuchsia.
Botanical name	*Fuchsia tripyhlla* 'Gartenmeister Bonstedt'.
Interesting facts	Named after the 14th-century German botanist Leonard Fuchs.
Origin	Haiti, San Domingo.
Position	Bright light away from direct sun.
Temperature	Minimum winter temperature 55F.
Watering	Water well during growing season keeping compost moist. Water sparingly during winter.
Feeding	Throughout growing season with potash-rich fertilizer.
Humidity	Mist leaves frequently during summer. Stand pots on damp gravel trays.
Re-potting	Re-pot every year in the spring.
Propagation	Softwood cuttings in spring.

Common names	Blood lily, Red Cape.
Botanical name	*Haemanthus natalensis.*
Interesting facts	Name derived from the Greek, *haima,* meaning blood, (alluding to the red colour of the flower), and *anthos,* a flower.
Origin	Natal, South Africa.
Position	Full sun.
Temperature	Minimum winter temperature 55F.
Watering	Compost must never be very wet, while during the winter it should be on the dry side.
Feeding	Throughout the growing season with potash-rich fertilizer.
Humidity	Place plants on a gravel tray and keep moist.
Re-potting	Only when necessary.
Propagation	Divide offsets at re-potting stage.

Common names	Heliotrope, Cherry pie.
Botanical name	*Heliotropium peruvianum (H. arborescens)*.
Interesting facts	Name derived from the Greek *helios*, the sun, and *trope*, to turn. An old belief has it that the flowers turn to the sun.
Origin	Peru.
Position	Well-lit position but shade from hot sun.
Temperature	Minimum winter temperature 40F.
Watering	Keep compost damp at all times. Reduce watering in the winter.
Feeding	Throughout growing season with potash-rich fertilizer.
Humidity	Mist occasionally.
Re-potting	Re-pot every year in the spring.
Propagation	Stem cutting in summer.

Common names	Guinea gold vine, Snake vine.
Botanical name	*Hibbertia scandens.*
Interesting facts	Named after a patron of botany, George Hibbert, who had a botanic garden at Clapham.
Origin	Queensland, New South Wales.
Position	Full sun.
Temperature	Minimum winter temperature 50F.
Watering	Water well throughout growing season, but allow compost to dry out between waterings.
Feeding	Throughout growing season with potash-rich fertilizer.
Humidity	Mist leaves occasionally or stand pots on damp gravel tray.
Re-potting	Re-pot when necessary in the spring.
Propagation	By seed or layering in the spring, or by cuttings in the summer.

Common name	Rose of China.
Botanical name	*Hibiscus rosa-sinensis.*
Interesting facts	*Hibiscus* is a Greek name of a very ancient origin used by the poet Virgil for a marrow-like plant.
Origin	Tropics and sub-tropics.
Position	Good well-lit position but out of direct sunlight.
Temperature	Minimum winter temperature 55F.
Watering	Keep moist at all times, but reduce slightly during the winter months.
Feeding	From April to September with a balanced houseplant fertilizer.
Humidity	Mist leaves occasionally or stand plants on a damp gravel tray.
Re-potting	May be necessary yearly in April.
Propagation	Stem cuttings in late spring.

Common name	Amaryllis.
Botanical name	*Hippeastrum hybrida.*
Interesting facts	From Greek, *hippeus,* a knight and *astron,* a star.
Origin	Central and South America.
Position	Full sun.
Temperature	Minimum winter temperature 50F.
Watering	Start watering when growth begins. Allow compost surface to dry out between waterings.
Feeding	During growing season with potash-rich fertilizer.
Humidity	Mist leaves occasionally.
Re-potting	Every 3–5 years.
Propagation	Offsets at re-potting time.

Common names	Chinese jasmine, Pink jasmine.
Botanical name	*Jasminum polyanthum.*
Interesting facts	Extremely fragrant flowers in the spring. *Polyanthum* means 'many flowered'. The name *Jasminum* is said to be derived from *ysmyn,* an Arabic name for jasmine.
Origin	Western China.
Position	Well-lit position with some direct light.
Temperature	Minimum winter temperature 45F.
Watering	Keep compost moist at all times.
Feeding	Throughout growing season with potash-rich fertilizer.
Humidity	Mist leaves often and stand pots on a damp gravel tray.
Re-potting	Re-pot when necessary.
Propagation	By stem cuttings in the spring.

Common name	Flaming Katy.
Botanical name	*Kalanchoe blossfeldiana.*
Interesting facts	*Kalanchoe* is the Latinized form of the Chinese name of one species.
Origin	Malagasy.
Position	During growing season in east - or west-facing windowsill, during the winter months on a south-facing windowsill.
Temperature	Minimum winter temperature of 50F.
Watering	Water well, but allow surface of compost to dry out between waterings.
Feeding	Throughout growing season with potash-rich fertilizer.
Humidity	This plant will tolerate a dry atmosphere.
Re-potting	Every year in the spring.
Propagation	From seeds or cuttings in the spring.

Common name	Kalanchoe.
Botanical name	*Kalanchoe uniflora (Bryophyllum uniflorum).*
Interesting facts	*Kalanchoe* is the Latinized form of the Chinese name for one species, and *uniflora* means one-flowered.
Origin	Malagasy.
Position	Full sun.
Temperature	Minimum winter temperature 55F.
Watering	Water thoroughly, then allow compost surface to dry before watering again. Reduce watering in winter.
Feeding	Feed throughout growing season with potash-rich fertilizer.
Humidity	This plant can tolerate a dry atmosphere.
Re-potting	Re-pot in spring after the plant's winter rest.
Propagation	From seed.

Common name	Cape cowslip.
Botanical name	*Lachenalia aloides (L. tricolor).*
Interesting facts	Named after Werner de la Chenal, Professor of Botany at Basle University.
Origin	Cape.
Position	Well-lit with some full sun.
Temperature	Minimum winter temperature of 45F.
Watering	Keep compost moist at all times during flowering and continue for several weeks, then gradually reduce amount and stop.
Feeding	Feed with potash-rich fertilizer throughout growing season.
Humidity	Mist leaves occasionally.
Re-potting	Re-pot every September.
Propagation	Remove offsets and re-plant in September.

Common name	Banana.
Botanical name	*Musa.*
Interesting facts	The name is of doubtful origin, possibly honouring Antonius Musa, a freedman of Emperor Augustus. The Arabic and Egyptian name is Mauz and this is considered by some to be the basis of the Latin *Musa.*
Origin	Tropical Asia and East Africa.
Position	Well-lit but out of direct sunlight.
Temperature	Minimum winter temperature of 66F.
Watering	During growing season ensure that compost is moist at all times. During winter allow the surface to dry before watering again.
Feeding	With a well-balanced fertilizer throughout the growing season.
Humidity	Occasionally mist the leaves.
Re-potting	When necessary.
Propagation	By division, offsets or suckers when potting or by seed in spring.

Common names	Oleander, Rose-bay.
Botanical name	*Nerium oleander.*
Interesting facts	*Nerium* is the ancient Greek name for oleander. This plant contains poisonous sap but has fragrant flowers.
Origin	Mediterranean region, across Asia to Japan.
Position	Full sun.
Temperature	Minimum winter temperature of 45F.
Watering	Water well during the growing season, but just keep damp in the winter months.
Feeding	Throughout growing season with potash-rich fertilizer.
Humidity	Do not mist leaves. This plant will tolerate a dry atmosphere.
Re-potting	Re-pot when necessary in the spring.
Propagation	Stem cuttings in the spring or summer or from seeds in the spring.

Common names Passion flower, Banana passion fruits.

Botanical name *Passiflora exonensis.*

Interesting facts *Passiflora* derives from the Latin *passio,* passion and *flos,* a flower. From the linking of the flower, by Jesuit missionaries, to the Passion of Christ.

Origin Garden origin. A hybrid between *P. antioquiensis x mollissima.*

Position Full sun.

Temperature Minimum winter temperature 40–50F.

Watering Daily watering may be necessary in the summer to keep the compost moist. Reduce the amount during winter.

Feeding Throughout the growing season with a potash-rich fertilizer.

Humidity Mist leaves occasionally.

Re-potting When necessary.

Propagation Cuttings in the spring.

Common name	Geranium.
Botanical name	*Pelargonium hortorum* hybrid.
Interesting facts	Seed head is said to resemble the head of a stork. Greek *pelargos*, a stork.
Origin	Africa, Atlantic Islands, eastwards to Arabia and South India, also in Australasia.
Position	Direct sunlight is necessary for good growth.
Temperature	Minimum winter temperature of 45F.
Watering	Water well, then leave compost to dry between waterings. During winter keep compost barely moist.
Feeding	From April to September with a potash-rich fertilizer.
Humidity	Misting is not necessary and may cause petal marking if carried out when the plant is in flower.
Re-potting	When necessary in the spring.
Propagation	Stem tip cuttings in the spring and summer. Do not use hormone rooting compounds.

Common names	Cape leadwort, Blue Cape.
Botanical name	*Plumbago capensis.*
Interesting facts	*Plumbago* from the Latin *plumbum*, lead, named by the Roman Pliny who attributed the curing of lead disease to the European species.
Origin	Widespread in the warmer regions of the world.
Position	Bright well-lit position with some direct light.
Temperature	Minimum winter temperature of 45F.
Watering	During the growing season keep the compost moist at all times. Water sparingly in the winter.
Feeding	From April to September with a general liquid fertilizer.
Humidity	Mist frequently.
Re-potting	When necessary in the spring.
Propagation	Seed sown in the spring or stem cuttings in the autumn.

Common names	Poor man's orchid, Butterfly flower.
Botanical name	*Schizanthus* hybrida.
Interesting facts	From the Greek, *schizo,* to cut, and *anthos,* a flower. The flowers have deeply fringed petals.
Origin	Garden hybrid.
Position	Well-lit in direct sun.
Temperature	Minimum winter temperature of 50–60F.
Watering	Keep moist at all times.
Feeding	From April to September with a potash-rich fertilizer.
Humidity	Mist leaves occasionally or stand on damp gravel tray.
Re-potting	Normally grown as annuals and thrown away after flowering.
Propagation	Sow seed in the spring or autumn.

Common name	Cineraria.
Botanical name	*Senecio cruentus.*
Interesting facts	Name derived from Latin *cinereus* meaning ash - coloured, referring to the colour of the underside of the leaves.
Origin	Derived from species of *senecio* introduced during the 18th century from the Canaries.
Position	Bright light away from direct sunshine.
Temperature	45–55F is best to ensure long flowering period.
Watering	Water frequently with tepid water.
Feeding	8 weeks after potting start to feed with potash-rich fertilizer..
Humidity	Stand pot on saucer of pebbles and keep these moist.
Re-potting	Normally seed produced, pricked out, moved to 3.5 inch pot, then to 5 inch pot.
Propagation	Seed raised in May through to July in cool greenhouse.

Common names	Jacobean lily, Aztec lily.
Botanical name	*Sprekelia formosissima (Amaryllis formosissima).*
Interesting facts	Named after J. H. von Sprekelsen, a German lawyer, who sent the plant to Linnaeus, the person who classified plants.
Origin	Mexico.
Position	Well-lit.
Temperature	Minimum winter temperature of 45–50F.
Watering	Dry off leaves in autumn when they start going yellow. Plant in late winter or early spring leaving neck of bulb just above soil surface.
Feeding	Use balanced houseplant fertilizer in the spring.
Humidity	Place pots on a damp gravel tray.
Re-potting	In late winter or early spring.
Propagation	By offsets or seed.

Common name	Cape primrose.
Botanical name	*Streptocarpus* 'Lady Strathallen'.
Interesting facts	Name derived from Greek, *streptos*, twisted, and *karpos*, a fruit which is spiralled.
Origin	Garden hybrid.
Position	Brightly-lit spot away from direct sun in summer.
Temperature	Minimum winter temperature of 55F.
Watering	Water freely, but allow compost surface to dry between waterings. Water sparingly in winter.
Feeding	Every 2 weeks from April to September with potash-rich fertilizer.
Humidity	Stand plants on a damp gravel tray.
Re-potting	Re-pot every spring.
Propagation	Divide plants in the spring or take leaf sections cuttings in the summer. May also be raised from seed sown in the spring.

Common name	Black-eyed Susan.
Botanical name	*Thunbergia alata* 'Susie'.
Interesting facts	The plant is named after the Swedish botanist Karl P. Thunber who was a student of Linnaeus and travelled widely in South Africa.
Origin	Tropical Africa.
Position	A well-lit position in full sun.
Temperature	Minimum winter temperature of 55F.
Watering	Keep the compost moist at all times.
Feeding	Throughout growing season with a potash-rich fertilizer.
Humidity	Mist frequently and stand pot on damp gravel tray.
Re-potting	Normally grown as an annual and thrown away after flowering.
Propagation	From seed in early spring.

Common name	Yellow arum lily.
Botanical name	*Zantedeschia* 'Lady Luck'.
Interesting facts	Named after the Italian botanist Francesco Zantedischi.
Origin	Garden hybrid.
Position	A well-lit position with some direct light.
Temperature	Minimum winter temperature of 50F.
Watering	During the growing season keep the compost wet at all times.
Feeding	During the growing season with potash-rich fertilizer.
Humidity	Mist leaves occasionally.
Re-potting	After flowering reduce water and then stop altogether when the foliage turns yellow. Re-pot into fresh compost in the autumn.
Propagation	Division of the rhizome or pot up offsets at re-potting in the autumn.

Foliage Plants for Well-Lit Positions

Common names	Century plant, Maguey.
Botanical name	*Agave americana medio-picta.*
Interesting facts	The sap is fermented to produce the Mexican national drink pulque.
Origin	Mexico.
Position	Full sun especially in winter.
Temperature	Minimum winter temperature of 45F.
Watering	Water like a normal houseplant during the summer, in the autumn reduce the amount and by October keep almost dry.
Feeding	Feed with a balanced houseplant fertilizer from May to August.
Humidity	Do not mist and give plenty of ventilation.
Re-potting	Only when necessary.
Propagation	Seed sown in the spring, re-pot divisions when necessary.

Common name	Common pineapple.
Botanical name	*Ananas comosus variegatus.*
Interesting facts	Name derived from South American name for pineapple – *nanas.*
Origin	Tropics of Central and South America.
Position	Full sun.
Temperature	Minimum winter temperature of 50F.
Watering	Never over-water and ensure there is good drainage, but keep compost moist.
Feeding	Every 2 weeks with potash-rich fertilizer.
Humidity	Mist leaves occasionally, or stand plant on damp gravel tray.
Re-potting	Only when pot-bound.
Propagation	By offsets, from base of plant.

Common name	Iron Cross Begonia.
Botanical name	*Begonia masoniana.*
Interesting facts	Named after Mr L. Maurice Mason. Common name is said to refer to the brown pattern on the leaf which resembles the German Iron Cross.
Origin	South-East Asia.
Position	A well-lit position out of direct sunlight. Turn plant frequently to prevent one-sided growth.
Temperature	Minimum winter temperature of 55F.
Watering	Keep compost moist from April to October then reduce over winter, allowing surface of compost to dry between waterings.
Feeding	Feed from April to October with a balanced houseplant fertilizer.
Humidity	A moist atmosphere is essential or brown leaf margins occur. Stand plant on a damp gravel tray and mist leaves frequently.
Re-potting	Re-pot each spring if necessary.
Propagation	By division.

Common names	Flame nettle, Painted nettle.
Botanical name	*Coleus blumei.*
Interesting facts	Name derived from the Greek *koleos*, a sheath, referring to the stamens being united to enclose the style. Named after Carl Ludwig von Blume.
Origin	Tropical Africa and Asia.
Position	Well-lit position but out of direct sunlight.
Temperature	Minimum winter temperature of 50F.
Watering	During growing season keep moist at all times, reduce watering in the winter.
Feeding	Feed with a nitrogen-rich fertilizer from April to September.
Humidity	Maintain a moist atmosphere at all times. Stand plant on a damp gravel tray.
Re-potting	Cut back growth in February or March and re-pot each season.
Propagation	Sow seeds in February or March or from stem cutting in spring or summer.

Common name	Jade plant.
Botanical name	*Crassula argentea (C.portulacea).*
Interesting facts	Name derived from the Latin *crassus,* thick. referring to the thick or fleshy leaves of the plant.
Origin	Nomaqualand to Transvaal.
Position	Well-lit but out of direct sunlight.
Temperature	Minimum winter temperature of 45F.
Watering	Water well throughout growing season, but keep on the dry side during winter.
Feeding	Throughout the growing season with a well-balanced houseplant fertilizer.
Humidity	This plant will tolerate a dry atmosphere.
Re-potting	Only re-pot when necessary. Produces a better plant when grown in a shallow container rather than a deep one.
Propagation	Stem cuttings in the spring.

Common names	Golden barrel, Golden ball.
Botanical name	*Echinocactus grusonii.*
Interesting facts	Named after Herman Gruson who owned a large collection of cacti. Name derived from Greek *echinos,* meaning hedgehog.
Origin	Central Mexico.
Position	Full sun especially in the winter months.
Temperature	Minimum winter temperature of 45F.
Watering	Water like a normal houseplant from May to August. In the autumn reduce amount and by October keep almost dry.
Feeding	Feed with balanced houseplant fertilizer from May to August.
Humidity	Do not mist and give plenty of ventilation.
Re-potting	Only re-pot when absolutely necessary.
Propagation	Sow seeds in spring.

Common names	Purple passion vine, Purple velvet plant.
Botanical name	*Gynura sarmentosa.*
Interesting facts	Named from the Greek *gyne,* female and *oura,* a tail, a reference to the long stigma.
Origin	From Malaya to the Philippines.
Position	Good well-lit position in full sun.
Temperature	Minimum winter temperature of 50F.
Watering	Keep moist during the growing season, then reduce the amount in winter.
Feeding	Feed once a month throughout the growing season with a well-balanced houseplant fertilizer.
Humidity	Only the occasional misting is necessary.
Re-potting	Re-pot in the spring if necessary.
Propagation	Stem cuttings from April to August.

Common names	Polka dot plant, Freckle face, Baby's tears.
Botanical name	*Hypoestes phyllostachya.*
Interesting facts	The common name freckle face refers to the pink spots on the leaves.
Origin	Malagasy.
Position	Well-lit in full sun.
Temperature	Minimum winter temperature of 55F.
Watering	The compost should be moist during the growing season, but reduce the amount in winter and keep on the dry side.
Feeding	Throughout the growing season with a nitrogen-rich fertilizer.
Humidity	Mist the leaves frequently and stand pot on a damp gravel tray.
Re-potting	May be necessary every spring.
Propagation	Sow seeds in the spring or propagate from stem cuttings in the summer.

Common name	Beefsteak plant.
Botanical name	*Iresine herbstii.*
Interesting facts	Named after Hermann Carl Gottlieb Herbst, director of the Rio de Janeiro Botanic Gardens.
Origin	South America.
Position	Well-lit but out of direct sunlight.
Temperature	Minimum winter temperature of 55F.
Watering	Keep the compost moist at all times but reduce the amount of watering in winter.
Feeding	Feed with a nitrogen-rich fertilizer from April to September.
Humidity	Stand plant on a damp gravel tray.
Re-potting	Re-pot every spring if necessary.
Propagation	Stem cuttings in the summer months.

Common names	Sensitive plant, Touch-me-not, Humble plant.
Botanical name	*Mimosa pudica.*
Interesting facts	Name derived from the Greek *mimos*, a mimic, a reference to the plant leaves which fold down when touched.
Origin	Tropical America.
Position	Well-lit but out of direct sunlight.
Temperature	Minimum winter temperature of 60F.
Watering	Keep moist during the growing season but reduce watering in winter.
Feeding	Throughout the season with a well-balanced houseplant fertilizer.
Humidity	Stand plant on a damp gravel tray.
Re-potting	Only when necessary in April.
Propagation	Seeds may be difficult to germinate: pour hot water over them before sowing in the early spring.

Common name	Bromeliad.
Botanical name	*Neoregelia carolinae, Nidularium meyendorfii, Aregelia marechalii.*
Interesting facts	Plants may be grown on moss poles or moss trees.
Origin	Brazil.
Position	Well-lit but out of direct sunlight.
Temperature	Minimum winter temperature of 50F.
Watering	Into the rosette of the leaves using rainwater. Only water the compost when this dries out. Empty and refill central rosette every month.
Feeding	Feed from April to September with a well-balanced houseplant fertilizer onto the compost. Ensure the compost is moist before feeding.
Humidity	Mist the leaves frequently in the summer.
Re-potting	Rarely necessary except when plants become top heavy, then re-pot in the spring.
Propagation	Offsets removed in the spring.

Common name	Castor oil plant.
Botanical name	*Ricinus communis.*
Interesting facts	Name derived from the Latin *ricinus,* a tick. The seed is said to resemble a tick.
Origin	Africa.
Position	Well-lit, will tolerate full sun.
Temperature	Minimum winter temperature of 50F.
Watering	Water well during growing season but reduce the amount in winter.
Feeding	Feed with balanced houseplant fertilizer every 2 weeks from April to September.
Humidity	Mist leaves occasionally.
Re-potting	Re-pot every spring if necessary. The plant is frequently grown as an annual.
Propagation	By seed in the spring.

Flowering Plants for Partial or Semi-Shaded Positions

Common names	Urn plant, Vase plant, Silver vase.
Botanical name	*Aechmea fasciata*.
Interesting facts	Name derived from Greek *aichme*, a point, a reference to the rigid parts on the flowers in the bud stage.
Origin	Brazil.
Position	Semi-shade.
Temperature	Minimum winter temperature of 50F.
Watering	Ensure central vase is filled with water, just keep the compost moist.
Feeding	Only occasionally onto the compost, ensuring this is moist before feeding.
Humidity	Mist leaves frequently in the summer.
Re-potting	Only when necessary.
Propagation	By offsets produced in the spring.

Common names	Coral berry, Spiceberry.
Botanical name	*Ardisia crispa*.
Interesting facts	Name derived from the Greek *ardis*, a point. The anthers are spear-shaped.
Origin	South-East Asia.
Position	Semi-shade.
Temperature	Minimum winter temperature of 45F.
Watering	Keep moist at all times during the summer but reduce amount in winter.
Feeding	Feed every 2 weeks from April to September with a nitrogen-rich fertilizer.
Humidity	Mist leaves frequently and stand pot on a damp gravel tray.
Re-potting	When necessary in the spring.
Propagation	Seed sown in the early spring or from cuttings in the summer.

Common name	Trailing Begonia.
Botanical name	*Begonia sutherlandii.*
Interesting facts	The plants were named after the French botanist Michael Begon.
Origin	South Africa.
Position	Semi-shade.
Temperature	Minimum winter temperature of 50F.
Watering	Water well during growing season but allow surface of compost to dry out between waterings.
Feeding	During the growing season with a potash-rich fertilizer.
Humidity	Mist leaves occasionally.
Re-potting	In the spring when necessary.
Propagation	By division.

Common name	Orchid.
Botanical name	*Brassia brachiata (B. verrucosa).*
Interesting facts	Brassia was named for William Bass who collected plants in West Africa for Sir Joseph Banks, who became a close friend of King George III and unofficial director of the Royal Botanic Gardens, Kew.
Origin	Mexico to Venezuela.
Position	Semi-shade.
Temperature	Minimum winter temperature of 55F.
Watering	Water well during the growing season, but allow surface of the compost to dry out between waterings. Reduce amount in winter.
Feeding	Feed with orchid fertilizer according to manufacturer's recommendations.
Humidity	Mist leaves occasionally.
Re-potting	In the spring if necessary into specialized orchid compost.
Propagation	By division.

Common name	Yesterday, today and tomorrow.
Botanical name	*Brunsfelsia latifolia (Franciscea latifolia).*
Interesting facts	Named after Otto Brunfels, a German monk and botanist.
Origin	Tropical Central and South America.
Position	Semi-shade.
Temperature	Minimum winter temperature of 50F.
Watering	Water frequently during the growing season but reduce the amount during the winter months.
Feeding	Throughout the growing season at 14-day intervals with a balanced fertilizer.
Humidity	Mist leaves frequently during the summer.
Re-potting	Re-pot if necessary in the spring.
Propagation	Stem cuttings in the summer months.

Common name	Camellia.
Botanical name	*Camellia* 'Inspiration'.
Interesting facts	Named after George Joseph Kamel, a pharmacist who studied the flora of the Philippines.
Origin	Garden origin.
Position	Semi-shade.
Temperature	Minimum winter temperature of 45F.
Watering	During the growing season keep moist at all times, reduce amount in the winter months.
Feeding	From April to September with a potash-rich fertilizer.
Humidity	Mist leaves occasionally.
Re-potting	Re-pot every spring, if necessary into compost which does not contain lime.
Propagation	Stem cuttings in the spring.

Common name	Cestrum.
Botanical name	*Cestrum elegans (Cestrum purpureum).*
Interesting facts	*Cestrum* is from the Greek word for an unknown species, used by Linnaeus.
Origin	Mexico.
Position	Semi-shade.
Temperature	Minimum winter temperature of 45F.
Watering	During the growing season keep moist. Reduce amount in winter.
Feeding	Feed throughout growing season with a potash-rich fertilizer.
Humidity	Mist leaves occasionally.
Re-potting	Re-pot when necessary in the spring.
Propagation	Stem cuttings in the spring.

Common name	Goldfish plant.
Botanical name	*Columnea gloriosa.*
Interesting facts	Named after Fabius Columna, an Indian botanist and author of the first work to use copperplate illustrations.
Origin	Costa Rica.
Position	Semi-shade.
Temperature	Minimum winter temperature of 50F.
Watering	During the growing season keep the compost moist at all times. Water sparingly during winter.
Feeding	Feed throughout the growing season with a potash-rich fertilizer.
Humidity	Mist leaves frequently, surround pot with damp peat to maintain humidity.
Re-potting	Every 2–3 years in the spring.
Propagation	By stem cutting after flowering.

Common name	Florists' Cyclamen.
Botanical name	*Cyclamen persicum.*
Interesting facts	Derived from the Greek name *Kyklaminos,* from *kyklos,* a circle, referring to the coiled stem of the seed head.
Origin	Southern and eastern regions of the Mediterranean from Algeria to Lebanon, and some Greek islands.
Position	Semi-shade.
Temperature	Minimum winter temperature of 50F.
Watering	Keep compost moist at all times, ensuring that the compost does not dry out.
Feeding	Weekly with a potash-rich fertilizer until the flowers form.
Humidity	Stand pot on a damp gravel tray or surround pot with peat and keep damp.
Re-potting	July into fresh compost. Then start tuber into growth.
Propagation	Seeds sown in July may take up to 12–18 months to flower.

Common name	Angels' trumpet.
Botanical name	*Datura x candida* 'Plena'.
Interesting facts	*Datura* is the Latin version of the Hindustani *dhatura*, or possibly of the Arabic *tatorah*. The plant has very sweetly scented flowers.
Origin	Garden origin. A hybrid between *D. aurea* and *D. versicolor*.
Position	Semi-shade.
Temperature	Minimum winter temperature of 50F.
Watering	Water well during the growing season, keeping compost moist at all times. Reduce the amount in winter.
Feeding	Throughout growing season with a potash-rich fertilizer every 2 weeks from April until September.
Humidity	Mist leaves occasionally.
Re-potting	Re-pot each spring if necessary.
Propagation	By cuttings in late spring and summer.

Common name	Pineapple flower.
Botanical name	*Eucomis comosa (E. punctata).*
Interesting facts	Name derived from the Greek *eu,* good and *kome,* hair. The effect of the leaves resembles a good head of hair.
Origin	South Africa.
Position	Semi-shade.
Temperature	Minimum winter temperature of 45F.
Watering	Water well during the growing season, but allow compost surface to dry out between waterings. Reduce the amount in winter.
Feeding	Every 2 weeks in the growing season with a potash-rich fertilizer.
Humidity	Mist leaves occasionally.
Re-potting	Re-pot every year in the spring.
Propagation	Remove offsets in the spring or sow seeds in the spring.

Common name	Persian violet.
Botanical name	*Exacum affine.*
Interesting facts	Name derived from *exacon,* the Gallic name for *Centaurium,* used by Linnaeus for the genus.
Origin	Socotra (Indian Ocean).
Position	Semi-shade.
Temperature	Minimum winter temperature of 50F.
Watering	Keep the compost moist at all times.
Feeding	Throughout growing season with a potash-rich fertilizer.
Humidity	Stand plants on damp gravel tray and mist leaves frequently.
Re-potting	Normally the plant is thrown away after flowering.
Propagation	Sow seeds in summer.

Common name	Kahili ginger.
Botanical name	*Hedychium gardnerianum.*
Interesting facts	The generic name refers to the first species described. In Greek *hedys* means sweet and *chion* snow and the first species had pure white sweet-smelling flowers.
Origin	Northern India.
Position	Semi-shade.
Temperature	Minimum winter temperature of 50F.
Watering	Water well during the growing season keeping the compost moist at all times. During the winter reduce the amount of water.
Feeding	Every 2 weeks throughout the growing season with a potash-rich fertilizer.
Humidity	Mist leaves frequently.
Re-potting	Every spring if necessary.
Propagation	By division in the spring.

Common name	Common Hydrangea.
Botanical name	*Hydrangea macrophylla (H. hortensis).*
Interesting facts	Name derived from Greek *hydro,* water, and *aggos,* a jar, making reference to the tiny cup-shaped seed capsules.
Origin	Japan.
Position	Semi-shade.
Temperature	Minimum winter temperature of 45F.
Watering	During the growing season keep moist at all times. Reduce the amount over winter. If water contains lime use rainwater.
Feeding	Throughout growing season with a potash-rich fertilizer every 2 weeks.
Humidity	Mist leaves occasionally.
Re-potting	Every spring if necessary, or treat as a short-term pot plant and plant into garden after flowering.
Propagation	Stem cutting in the spring.

Common name	Busy Lizzie.
Botanical name	*Impatiens* 'New Guinea Hybrids'.
Interesting facts	Name derived from the Latin *impatiens*, meaning impatient, referring to the way the seed explodes and scatters from some species.
Origin	Garden origin.
Position	Semi-shade.
Temperature	Minimum winter temperature of 55F.
Watering	Throughout the growing season keep moist at all times. Reduce the amount in winter.
Feeding	Every week throughout the growing season with a potash-rich fertilizer.
Humidity	Mist the leaves occasionally, but not when the plant is in flower.
Re-potting	Only when pot-bound in the spring. Over-potting results in foliage growth at the expense of flowers.
Propagation	Seeds or cuttings in the spring.

Common name	Lantana.
Botanical name	*Lanata sellowiana* *(L. montevidensis).*
Interesting facts	*Lantana* is an ancient name for viburnum, as the foliage of the 2 shrubs looks similar.
Origin	South America.
Position	Semi-shade.
Temperature	Minimum winter temperature of 55F.
Watering	Keep the compost moist throughout the growing season, allowing the surface to dry out between waterings. Reduce the amount in the winter, sparingly in the spring.
Feeding	Every 2 weeks throughout the growing season with a potash-rich fertilizer.
Humidity	Mist leaves occasionally.
Re-potting	Re-pot if necessary in the spring.
Propagation	Sow seeds in the spring or stem cuttings in the summer.

Common name	Chilean bell flower.
Botanical name	*Lapageria rosea.*
Interesting facts	Named after Josephine de la Pagerie, Napoleon's Empress.
Origin	Central Chile.
Position	Semi-shade.
Temperature	Minimum winter temperature of 40F.
Watering	Allow compost surface to dry out between waterings.
Feeding	Every 2 weeks throughout the growing season with a potash-rich fertilizer.
Humidity	Mist leaves occasionally.
Re-potting	Only when necessary.
Propagation	Sow seeds in the spring after soaking in water for 48 hours.

Common name	Pink allamanda.
Botanical name	*Mandevilla splendens (Dipladenia sanderi).*
Interesting facts	*Mandevilla* was named after Henry John Mandeville, a British minister in Argentina who introduced the first species into cultivation.
Origin	Brazil.
Position	Semi-shade.
Temperature	Minimum winter temperature of 55F.
Watering	Water regularly throughout the growing season, sparingly during winter.
Feeding	Every 2 weeks throughout the growing season with a balanced houseplant fertilizer.
Humidity	Mist plant regularly especially when buds are forming and stand plant on a damp gravel tray.
Re-potting	Re-pot every year in the spring.
Propagation	Stem cutting in the spring.

Common name	Peristrophe.
Botanical name	*Peristrophe speciosa.*
Interesting facts	Name derived from the Greek *peri,* around and *strophe,* twist, referring to the twisted corolla lobes.
Origin	India.
Position	Semi-shade.
Temperature	Minimum winter temperature of 50F.
Watering	Water well throughout growing season but allow the compost surface to dry out between waterings. Reduce the amount during the winter.
Feeding	Every 2 weeks throughout growing season with balanced houseplant fertilizer.
Humidity	Mist leaves occasionally.
Re-potting	When necessary in the spring.
Propagation	Stem cuttings in the spring.

Common name	Fairy primrose.
Botanical name	*Primula malacoides.*
Interesting facts	*Malacoides* means mallow-like.
Origin	Western China.
Position	Semi-shade.
Temperature	Minimum winter temperature of 55F.
Watering	Keep plants moist especially during the flowering period.
Feeding	Feed every 2 weeks throughout the growing season with a balanced houseplant fertilizer.
Humidity	Mist leaves occasionally and place plant on a damp gravel tray.
Re-potting	Normally grown as an annual and potted into a 3.5 inch pot then into a 5 inch pot and thrown away after flowering is completed.
Propagation	Seeds sown in June or July.

Common name	African violet.
Botanical name	*Saintpaulia ionantha.*
Interesting facts	Named after Baron Walter von Saint Paul Illaire, who found the first species.
Origin	Coastal Tanzania.
Position	Semi-shade, but well-lit spot during the winter months. For winter blooms 14 hours of artificial light is necessary.
Temperature	Minimum winter temperature of 55F.
Watering	Keep compost moist, but allow surface of compost to dry between waterings. Reduce amount of watering during the winter months.
Feeding	Every 2 weeks with a specialist *Saintpaulia* fertilizer.
Humidity	Do not wet foliage, place plant on a damp gravel tray.
Re-potting	Re-pot if necessary in the spring.
Propagation	Leaf cuttings in the spring or sow seeds.

Common name	Christmas cactus.
Botanical name	*Schlumbergia x buckleyi.*
Interesting facts	Named after Frederick Schlumberger, a Belgian grower, explorer and plant collector.
Origin	Garden hybrid.
Position	Semi-shade.
Temperature	Minimum winter temperature of 55F.
Watering	Water well throughout the growing season, allowing the surface to dry out between waterings. Just keep moist in the winter.
Feeding	Every 2 weeks throughout the growing season with a balanced houseplant fertilizer.
Humidity	Mist leaves frequently.
Re-potting	Annually once flowering has finished.
Propagation	Cuttings taken between April and August. Allow cuttings to dry before putting them into the compost.

Common names	Peace lily, White sails.
Botanical name	*Spathiphyllum wallisii.*
Interesting facts	Name derived from the Greek *spathe*, bract (looking like a flower) and *phyllon*, leaf, the spathes being leaf-like in shape.
Origin	Colombia and Venezuela.
Position	Semi-shade.
Temperature	Minimum winter temperature of 55F.
Watering	Keep compost moist during growing season, and reduce the amount in winter.
Feeding	Throughout growing season with a potash-rich fertilizer.
Humidity	Stand plant on a damp gravel tray.
Re-potting	Every year in the spring.
Propagation	Divide plant at re-potting time.

Common name	Bird of paradise flower.
Botanical name	*Strelitzia reginae.*
Interesting facts	Named after Charlotte of Mecklenburg-Strelitz, who became the queen of George III.
Origin	South Africa.
Position	Semi-shade.
Temperature	Minimum winter temperature of 55F.
Watering	Water well throughout the growing season. Allow surface of compost to dry out between waterings, sparingly in the winter.
Feeding	Once every month with a potash-rich fertilizer.
Humidity	Do not wet foliage. Stand plant on a damp gravel tray.
Re-potting	Re-pot every year in the spring if necessary.
Propagation	Division of plant in spring when re-potting.

Common name	Marmalade bush.
Botanical name	*Streptosolen jamesonii.*
Interesting facts	Named derived from Greek *streptos*, twisted and *solen*, a tube, referring to the twisted corolla tubes.
Origin	Colombia, Ecuador.
Position	Semi-shade.
Temparature	Minimum winter temperature of 50F.
Watering	Water well throughout growing season. Allow the surface of the compost to dry between waterings and reduce the amount in winter.
Feeding	Every 2 weeks throughout the growing season with a potash-rich fertilizer.
Humidity	Mist leaves occasionally.
Re-potting	In the spring if necessary.
Propagation	Cuttings of young shoots in the late spring.

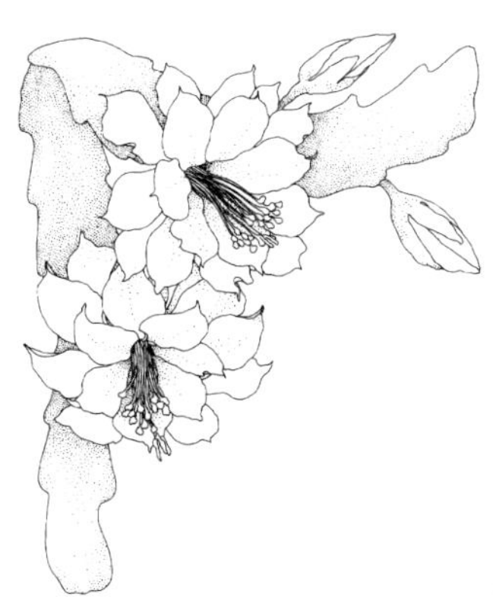

Foliage Plants for Semi-Shaded Positions

Common name	Chinese evergreen.
Botanical name	*Aglanonema* 'Silver Queen'.
Interesting facts	Name derived from the Greek *aglaos*, bright and *nema*, a thread, referring to the stamens. Grows best in a shallow pot.
Origin	Garden origin.
Position	Semi-shade.
Temperature	Minimum winter temperature of 60F.
Watering	During growing season water well, at other times of the year water sparingly.
Feeding	Every 2 weeks throughout the growing season with a nitrogen-rich houseplant fertilizer.
Humidity	Stand plant on a damp gravel tray and mist frequently.
Re-potting	Normally on a 3-year basis in the spring.
Propagation	Division in the spring.

Common name	Plume asparagus.
Botanical name	*Asparagus densiflorus (A. meyeri).*
Interesting facts	Name said to be derived from the Greek *intensive*, and *sparasso*, to tear, alluding to the prickles of some species.
Origin	South Africa.
Position	Semi-shade.
Temperature	Minimum winter temperature of 50F.
Watering	Best watered from base, regularly from spring to autumn but sparingly during winter.
Feeding	Every 2 weeks throughout the growing season with a nitrogen-rich houseplant fertilizer.
Humidity	Mist leaves occasionally.
Re-potting	Re-pot annually in the spring.
Propagation	Division in the spring or seeds in the spring.

Common name	Begonia.
Botanical name	*Begonia* Caribbean Hybrid.
Interesting facts	The genus was named after Michael Begon, patron of botany and once governor of French Canada.
Origin	Garden hybrid.
Position	Semi-shade.
Temperature	Minimum winter temperature of 55F.
Watering	Keep compost moist during the growing season but allow the compost to dry out between waterings. Water sparingly in the winter.
Feeding	Every 2 weeks throughout the growing season with a nitrogen-rich houseplant fertilizer.
Humidity	Stand plant on a damp gravel tray. Do not mist the leaves.
Re-potting	Annually in the spring.
Propagation	Division in the spring.

Common names	Spider plant, St Bernard's lily.
Botanical name	*Chlorophytum comosus variegatum (Anthericum comosus).*
Interesting facts	Name derived from Greek, *clideios,* delicate and *anthos,* a flower or *phytum,* a plant.
Origin	South Africa.
Position	Semi-shade.
Temperature	Minimum winter temperature of 45F.
Watering	Water well during the growing season, reduce the amount in winter.
Feeding	Every 2 weeks throughout the growing season with a nitrogen-rich houseplant fertilizer.
Humidity	Mist leaves occasionally.
Re-potting	Each spring.
Propagation	Peg down plantlets into compost when these are produced, cut through stem when rooted, or divide plants in the spring.

Common name	Ti tree.
Botanical name	*Cordyline terminalis* 'Kiwi'.
Interesting facts	*Cordyline* derives from *cordyle,* a club, referring to the swollen stem bases of some species which result in a somewhat club-like appearance.
Origin	Tropical Asia, Polynesia.
Position	Semi-shade.
Temperature	Minimum winter temperature of 55F.
Watering	Keep compost moist at all times, reduce the amount in the winter, but do not dry off completely.
Feeding	Every 2 weeks throughout the growing season with a nitrogen-rich houseplant fertilizer.
Humidity	Mist leaves frequently.
Re-potting	When necessary.
Propagation	Suckers detached in the late spring, or 2 inch long sections of stem in early summer, treat as cuttings.

Common names	Finger aralia, False aralia.
Botanical name	*Dizygotheca elegantissima (Aralia elegantissima).*
Interesting facts	Named from Greek *dis*, twice, *zygos*, a yoke and *theka*, a case. The anthers have four lobes, twice the normal number.
Origin	New Caledonia, Polynesia, Australasia.
Position	Semi-shade.
Temperature	Minimum winter temperature of 60F.
Watering	Only moderately during the growing season. Keep on the dry side during winter.
Feeding	Every 2 weeks throughout the growing season with a nitrogen-rich houseplant fertilizer.
Humidity	Stand plant on a damp gravel tray and mist leaves frequently.
Re-potting	Every 2 years in the spring.
Propagation	From imported seeds in the spring, or by air-layering. In the summer by stem section cuttings.

Common name	False palm.
Botanical name	*Dracaena deremensis* 'Yellow'.
Interesting facts	Name derived from the Greek *drakainia*, a dragon. Also suggested that it was named after Sir Francis Drake.
Origin	Tropical Africa.
Position	Semi-shade.
Temperature	Minimum winter temperature of 55F.
Watering	Keep the compost moist at all times. Reduce the amount during winter, but do not allow to dry out completely.
Feeding	Every 2 weeks throughout the growing season with a nitrogen-rich houseplant fertilizer.
Humidity	Mist leaves frequently.
Re-potting	Every 2 years.
Propagation	Stem section cuttings in the spring or stem tip cuttings in late spring .

Common name	Ribbon plant.
Botanical name	*Dracaena sanderiana.*
Interesting facts	See *Dracaena deremensis* p94.
Origin	Central Africa.
Position	Semi-shade.
Temperature	Minimum winter temperature of 55F.
Watering	See *D. deremensis.*
Feeding	Every 2 weeks throughout the growing season with a nitrogen-rich houseplant fertilizer.
Humidity	Mist the leaves frequently and stand plant on a damp gravel tray.
Re-potting	Every 2 years.
Propagation	Stem cuttings in the spring or stem tip cuttings in the late spring.

Common name	False castor-oil plant.
Botanical name	*Fatsia japonica (Aralia japonica, A. sieboldii).*
Interesting facts	*Fatsia* is the Latinized version of *fatsi*, said to be the Japanese name for the plant.
Origin	Japan, South Korea.
Position	Semi-shade.
Temperature	Minimum winter temperature of 40F.
Watering	Water frequently in the growing season but reduce the amount in winter.
Feeding	Every 2 weeks throughout the growing season with a nitrogen-rich houseplant fertilizer.
Humidity	Stand the plant on a damp gravel tray.
Re-potting	Every spring.
Propagation	From seeds in the late spring or stem cuttings in the summer.

Common name	Golden false castor-oil plant.
Botanical name	*Fatsia japonica* Gold.
Interesting facts	See *Fatsia japonica*.
Origin	Japan, South Korea.
Position	Semi-shade.
Temperature	Minimum winter temperature of 40F.
Watering	See *F. japonica*.
Feeding	Every 2 weeks throughout the growing season with a nitrogen-rich houseplant fertilizer.
Humidity	Stand plant on a damp gravel tray.
Re-potting	Every spring.
Propagation	Stem cuttings in the summer.

Common name	Weeping fig.
Botanical name	*Ficus benjamina.*
Interesting facts	Do not move the plant often or the leaves tend to drop off.
Origin	Tropical Asia.
Position	Semi-shade.
Temperature	Minimum winter temperature of 55F.
Watering	Water well but allow the surface of the compost to dry between waterings during the growing season. Reduce the amount in the winter.
Feeding	Every 2 weeks throughout the growing season with a nitrogen-rich houseplant fertilizer.
Humidity	Stand the plant on a damp gravel tray during the summer.
Re-potting	Only when necessary.
Propagation	Stem tip cuttings during the summer.

Common name	Rubber plant.
Botanical name	*Ficus elastica.*
Interesting facts	*Elastica* means producing elastic.
Origin	India, Malaysia.
Position	Semi-shade.
Temperature	Minimum winter temperature of 55F.
Watering	Water well during the growing season, but allow the surface of the compost to dry out between waterings. Reduce the amount in winter.
Feeding	Every 2 weeks throughout the growing season with a nitrogen-rich houseplant fertilizer.
Humidity	Stand the plant on a damp gravel tray.
Re-potting	Only when necessary.
Propagation	Air-layering in the summer, leaf bud cuttings or stem tip cuttings.

Common names	Rubber plant, Fig tree.
Botanical name	*Ficus elastica* 'Belga'.
Interesting facts	Fruits not normally produced on pot plants. The plants require plenty of space. *Fikus* is the Latin name for a fig tree. Believed to be from the Hebrew name, *Fag*.
Origin	India, Malaysia.
Position	Partially shaded.
Temperature	Minimum winter temperature 55F.
Watering	Allow compost to dry out between waterings. During the winter months just keep damp – not wet.
Feeding	From April to September with a balanced houseplant fertilizer.
Humidity	Mist leaves occasionally.
Re-potting	Plants grow better when slightly pot-bound. Re-pot every 2–3 years in the spring if necessary.
Propagation	Air-layer, leaf bud cuttings, stem cuttings.

Common names	Creeping fig, Climbing fig.
Botanical name	*Ficus pumila.*
Interesting facts	Normally grown as a creeping plant but also climbs.
Origin	Eastern Asia, Australia.
Position	Semi-shade.
Temperature	Minimum winter temperature of 55F.
Watering	Water well during the growing season, but reduce the amount in winter.
Feeding	Every 2 weeks throughout the growing season with a nitrogen-rich houseplant fertilizer.
Humidity	Stand the plant on a damp gravel tray and mist the leaves frequently.
Re-potting	Only when necessary.
Propagation	Stem tip cuttings in the summer.

Common name	Herringbone plant.
Botanical name	*Maranta* 'Tricolor', *M. leuconeura erythrophylla*.
Interesting facts	*Maranta* was named after Bartolommeo Maranti, an Italian physician and botanist.
Origin	Tropical America.
Position	Semi-shade.
Temperature	Minimum winter temperature of 50F.
Watering	Keep the compost moist during the growing season but allow the compost to dry out in winter.
Feeding	Every 2 weeks throughout the growing season with a nitrogen-rich houseplant fertilizer.
Humidity	Stand the plant on a damp gravel tray and mist the leaves frequently.
Re-potting	Only when necessary.
Propagation	Division in the spring.

Common names	Swiss cheese plant, Split leaf philodendron, Mexican bread fruit, Ceriman.
Botanical name	*Monstera deliciosa.*
Interesting facts	Derivation of first name is obscure, probably from *monstifer*, monster-bearing, referring to holes in plant leaves, which are large. Second name refers to the delicious fruits.
Origin	Mexico, Central America.
Position	Light shade.
Temperature	Active growth occurs at 65F, over winter at a minimum of 50F.
Watering	During November to March keep the soil moist; rest of the year water regularly ensuring pot is damp.
Feeding	Weekly from late March through to September with a balanced houseplant fertilizer.
Humidity	Mist leaves frequently throughout growing season. Wash dust off leaves occasionally.
Re-potting	Necessary every 2–3 years in April.
Propagation	Stem tip cuttings or air-layer.

Common name	Bead plant.
Botanical name	*Nertera granadensis.*
Interesting facts	*Nertera* derives from the Greek *nerteros,* lowly, referring to its low habit of growth.
Origin	Mexico and Central America.
Position	Semi-shade.
Temperature	Minimum winter temperature of 40F.
Watering	Keep compost moist during the growing season but reduce the amount in winter.
Feeding	Every 2 weeks throughout the growing season with a nitrogen-rich houseplant fertilizer.
Humidity	Mist the leaves occasionally.
Re-potting	Only when necessary, however the plant is normally thrown away after the beads have dropped off.
Propagation	Division in the spring.

Common name	Song of India.
Botanical name	*Pleomele reflexa variegata (Draceana reflexa).*
Interesting facts	*Reflexa* refers to the curled back flowers.
Origin	Madagascar, Mauritius.
Position	Semi-shade.
Temperature	Minimum winter temperature of 55F.
Watering	Keep the compost moist at all times. Reduce the amount in winter, but do not allow to dry out completely.
Feeding	Every 2 weeks throughout the growing season with a nitrogen-rich houseplant fertilizer.
Humidity	Mist leaves frequently.
Re-potting	Every 2 years.
Propagation	Stem section cuttings in the spring.

Common name	Radermachera.
Botanical name	*Radermachera sinica* 'Danielle' *(Stereospermum sinicum).*
Interesting facts	*Radermachera* commemorates J.C.M. Radermacher, a Dutch amateur botanist.
Origin	China.
Position	Semi-shade.
Temperature	Minimum winter temperature of 55F.
Watering	Keep compost moist at all times, but do not over-water in the winter.
Feeding	Every 2 weeks throughout the growing season with a nitrogen-rich houseplant fertilizer.
Humidity	This plant will tolerate a dry atmosphere, so misting is not necessary.
Re-potting	Only when necessary.
Propagation	By imported seed from China in summer.

Common name	Grape Ivy.
Botanical name	*Rhoicissus rhomboidea.*
Interesting facts	What is normally sold under this name is *Cissus rhombifolia,* as this species is not usually in cultivation.
Origin	South Africa.
Position	Semi-shade.
Temperature	Minimum winter temperature of 45F.
Watering	Water well during the growing season but reduce the amount in winter.
Feeding	Every 2 weeks throughout the growing season with a nitrogen-rich houseplant fertilizer.
Humidity	Mist the leaves occasionally.
Re-potting	When necessary in the spring.
Propagation	Stem cuttings in the spring or summer.

Common names	Mother-in-law's tongue, Snake plant.
Botanical name	*Sansevieria trifaciata laurentii.*
Interesting facts	The plant was named after Prince Raimond de Sanagrio de Sanseviero.
Origin	South Africa.
Position	Semi-shade.
Temperature	Minimum winter temperature of 50F.
Watering	Water moderately during the growing season, allowing the compost to dry between waterings, in winter only every 1–2 months.
Feeding	Every 2 weeks throughout the growing season with a nitrogen-rich houseplant fertilizer.
Humidity	This plant will tolerate a fairly dry atmosphere. Do not allow water to enter the heart of the plant.
Re-potting	This plant grows better if pot-bound, only re-pot when the roots crack the pot.
Propagation	By division in the spring.

Common names	Variegated mother of thousands, Strawberry geranium.
Botanical name	*Saxifraga sarmentosa* 'Tricolor' *(Saxifraga stolonifera).*
Interesting facts	The name reflects the habit of the plant in producing lots of overground stems.
Origin	Eastern Asia.
Position	Semi-shade.
Temperature	Minimum winter temperature of 40F.
Watering	Water well during the growing season. During the winter allow the surface of the compost to dry out between waterings.
Feeding	Every 2 weeks throughout the growing season with a nitrogen-rich houseplant fertilizer.
Humidity	Mist the leaves occasionally.
Re-potting	Every year in the spring.
Propagation	Peg down the plantlets during the growing season.

Common name	Stromanthe.
Botanical name	*Stomanthe amadilis, (Calathea amadilis, Maranta amabilis).*
Interesting facts	Named from the Greek *stroma*, a bed and *anthos*, a flower, reflecting the shape of the flower.
Origin	Brazil.
Position	Semi-shade.
Temperature	Minimum winter temperature of 50F.
Watering	Keep the compost moist throughout the growing season, but reduce the amount in winter.
Feeding	Every 2 weeks throughout the growing season with a nitrogen-rich houseplant fertilizer.
Humidity	Stand the pot on a damp gravel tray and mist the leaves frequently.
Re-potting	Every 2 years.
Propagation	Divide the plant in the spring.

Common name	Syngonium.
Botanical name	*Syngonium hoffmannii* hybrid *(Nephthytis hoffmannii).*
Interesting facts	*Syngonium* is derived from the Greek *syn,* together and *gone,* womb, an allusion to the united ovaries.
Origin	Garden origin.
Position	Semi-shade.
Temperature	Minimum winter temperature of 55F.
Watering	Keep the compost moist at all times during the growing season, but allow the surface of the compost to dry out between waterings in the winter.
Feeding	Every 2 weeks throughout the growing season with a nitrogen-rich houseplant fertilizer.
Humidity	Stand the pot on a damp gravel tray and mist the leaves frequently.
Re-potting	Every 2 years.
Propagation	Stem cuttings in the summer.

Common names	Goosefoot plant, Arrowhead vine.
Botanical name	*Syngonium podophyllum.*
Interesting facts	See *Syngonium hoffmannii* p111.
Origin	Mexico to Panama.
Position	Semi-shade.
Temperature	Minimum winter temperature of 55F.
Watering	See *S. hoffmannii.*
Feeding	Every 2 weeks throughout the growing season with a nitrogen-rich houseplant fertilizer.
Humidity	See *S. hoffmannii.*
Re-potting	Every 2 years.
Propagation	Stem cuttings in the summer.

Common names	Pick-a-back or Piggyback plant.
Botanical name	*Tolmiea menziesii.*
Interesting facts	Named after Dr William Fraser Tolmie, a surgeon to the Hudson Bay Company based in Fort Vancouver.
Origin	Western North America.
Position	Semi-shade.
Temperature	Minimum winter temperature of 40F.
Watering	Keep the compost moist during the growing season but reduce the amount in winter.
Feeding	Every 2 weeks throughout the growing season with a nitrogen-rich houseplant fertilizer.
Humidity	Mist the leaves occasionally.
Re-potting	Every year in the spring.
Propagation	Peg down the young plantlets during the summer.

Plants for Shaded Positions

Common name	Delta maidenhead fern.
Botanical name	*Adiantum raddianum (A. cuneatum, A. aemulum)*.
Interesting facts	Name derived from the Greek *adiantos*, dry or unwetted, referring to the water-repellent nature of the fronds.
Origin	Tropical America.
Position	Shade.
Temperature	Minimum winter temperature of 50F.
Watering	Never allow the compost to dry out – it should be moist but not soggy.
Feeding	Every 2 weeks throughout the growing season with a nitrogen-rich houseplant fertilizer.
Humidity	Stand the plant on a damp gravel tray and mist the leaves frequently.
Re-potting	Re-pot in spring only when necessary. Do not plant too deeply.
Propagation	Division of the plant in the spring or by spores.

Common names	Painter's palette, Tailflower.
Botanical name	*Anthurium andreanum.*
Interesting facts	Name derived from *anthos*, a flower and *oura*, tail, from the shape of the spadix.
Origin	Colombia.
Position	Shade.
Temperature	Minimum winter temperature of 60F.
Watering	Keep compost moist at all times, but do not allow compost to become soggy, especially during winter.
Feeding	Every 2 weeks throughout the growing season with a nitrogen-rich houseplant fertilizer.
Humidity	Stand the plant on a damp gravel tray and mist the leaves frequently.
Re-potting	When necessary in spring.
Propagation	Division in the spring.

Common name	Bird's nest fern.
Botanical name	*Asplenium nidus (A. nidus-avis).*
Interesting facts	Historically thought to have been used medicinally for curing problems with the spleen.
Origin	Tropical Asia, Australia.
Position	Shade.
Temperature	Minimum winter temperature of 50F.
Watering	Keep compost moist at all times, but do not allow to become soggy in winter.
Feeding	Every 2 weeks throughout the growing season with a nitrogen-rich houseplant fertilizer.
Humidity	Stand the plant on a damp gravel tray and mist the leaves frequently.
Re-potting	Only when necessary in the spring.
Propagation	Division in the spring or by spores.

Common names	Painted leaf, fan begonia.
Botanical name	*Begonia rex*.
Interesting facts	Most of the named forms with good leaf colour are garden hybrids.
Origin	Assam.
Position	Shade.
Temperature	Minimum winter temperature of 50F.
Watering	Keep moist during the growing season, but allow the surface of the compost to dry out between waterings in winter.
Feeding	Every 2 weeks throughout the growing season with a nitrogen-rich houseplant fertilizer.
Humidity	Stand the plant on a damp gravel tray and mist the leaves frequently.
Re-potting	Annually in the spring. Pot-bound plants lose their colour.
Propagation	Division of plants in the spring.

Common name	Angel's wings.
Botanical name	*Caladium hortulanum* 'Frieda Hemple'.
Interesting facts	Name derived from the vernacular name *Kaladi,* misused for this genus.
Origin	Garden origin.
Position	Shade.
Temperature	Minimum winter temperature of 60F.
Watering	Water well keeping compost moist during the growing season.
Feeding	Every 2 weeks throughout the growing season with a nitrogen-rich houseplant fertilizer.
Humidity	Stand the plant on a damp gravel tray and mist the leaves frequently.
Re-potting	Leaves die down in September. Stop watering and allow tubers to dry. Re-plant tubers in March and water well.
Propagation	By offsets or division of tubers in the spring.

Common name	Dumb cane.
Botanical name	*Dieffenbachia picta* 'Camilla' *(D. maculata).*
Interesting facts	The plant is poisonous and the sap should be kept away from skin, mouth and eyes.
Origin	Garden origin.
Position	Shade.
Temperature	Minimum winter temperature of 60F.
Watering	Water frequently during the growing season but allow the compost surface to dry out between waterings in winter.
Feeding	Every 2 weeks throughout the growing season with a nitrogen-rich houseplant fertilizer.
Humidity	Stand the plant on a damp gravel tray and mist the leaves frequently.
Re-potting	Every spring.
Propagation	Stem section cuttings.

Common name	Dumb cane.
Botanical name	*Dieffenbachia picta.*
Interesting facts	The plant is poisonous. Named after J. P. Diffenbach, the administrator of the Royal Palace Gardens in Vienna.
Origin	Brazil.
Position	Shade.
Temperature	Minimum winter temperature of 60F.
Watering	See *D. picta* 'Camilla'.
Feeding	Every 2 weeks throughout the growing season with a nitrogen-rich houseplant fertilizer.
Humidity	Stand the plant on a damp gravel tray and mist the leaves frequently.
Re-potting	Every spring.
Propagation	Stem section cuttings.

Common names	Painted net leaf, Nerve plant.
Botanical name	*Fittonia verschaffeltii* Red and Silver.
Interesting facts	*Fittonia* was named after Elizabeth and Sarah Mary Fitton who wrote *Conversations on Botany* in 1817.
Origin	Peru.
Position	Shade.
Temperature	Minimum winter temperature of 60F.
Watering	Water well during the growing season, but allow the surface of the compost to dry out between waterings in winter.
Feeding	Every 2 weeks throughout the growing season with a nitrogen-rich houseplant fertilizer.
Humidity	Stand the plant on a damp gravel tray and mist the leaves frequently.
Re-potting	Re-pot every spring.
Propagation	Division in the spring.

Common name	Ivy.
Botanical name	*Hedera helix.*
Interesting facts	*Helix* is thought to refer to the legend that the plant was wound around a staff carried by the wine-god Bacchus and his attendants.
Origin	Europe to the Caucasus.
Position	Shade.
Temperature	Minimum winter temperature of 45F.
Watering	Keep moist in the summer but allow surface of the compost to dry out between waterings in winter.
Feeding	Every 2 weeks throughout the growing season with a nitrogen-rich houseplant fertilizer.
Humidity	Stand the plant on a damp gravel tray and mist the leaves frequently.
Re-potting	When necessary in the spring.
Propagation	Cuttings in the spring.

Common name	Boston fern.
Botanical name	*Nephrolepsis exaltata 'Bostoniensis'.*
Interesting facts	Name derived from the Greek *nephros*, a kidney and *lepis*, a scale which covers the spores.
Origin	Garden origin.
Position	Shade.
Temperature	Minimum winter temperature of 50F.
Watering	Keep the compost moist at all times, but do not allow it to become soggy in winter.
Feeding	Every 2 weeks throughout the growing season with a nitrogen-rich houseplant fertilizer.
Humidity	Stand the plant on a damp gravel tray and mist the leaves frequently.
Re-potting	Only when necessary in the spring.
Propagation	By division or spores in the spring.

Common names	Sweetheart plant, Heart leaf.
Botanical name	*Philodendron scandens.*
Interesting facts	Name derived from the Greek *philos,* love and *dendron,* a tree.
Origin	Tropical America.
Position	Shade.
Temperature	Minimum winter temperature of 50F.
Watering	Water well during the growing season but keep compost just moist in the winter.
Feeding	Every 2 weeks throughout the growing season with a nitrogen-rich houseplant fertilizer.
Humidity	Stand the plant on a damp gravel tray and mist the leaves frequently.
Re-potting	Every 3 years.
Propagation	Cuttings in the spring.

Common name	Aluminium plant.
Botanical name	*Pilea cadierei.*
Interesting facts	*Pilea* derives from the Latin name *pileus,* a cap.
Origin	Vietnam.
Position	Shade.
Temperature	Minimum winter temperature of 50F.
Watering	Water well during the growing season but allow surface of the compost to dry out between waterings in winter.
Feeding	Every 2 weeks throughout the growing season with a nitrogen-rich houseplant fertilizer.
Humidity	Stand the plant on a damp gravel tray and mist the leaves frequently.
Re-potting	In the spring if necessary.
Propagation	Division in the spring or summer.

Common name	Staghorn fern.
Botanical name	*Platycerium bifurcatum (P. alcicorne).*
Interesting facts	Name derived from the Greek, *platys,* broad and *keros,* a horn, alluding to the shape of the fronds.
Origin	Eastern Australia to Polynesia.
Position	Shade.
Temperature	Minimum winter temperature of 50F.
Watering	Never allow the compost to dry out, but it should not be soggy in the winter.
Feeding	Every 2 weeks throughout the growing season with a nitrogen-rich houseplant fertilizer.
Humidity	Stand the plant on a damp gravel tray and mist the leaves frequently.
Re-potting	Only when necessary.
Propagation	Division in the summer .

Common name	Sword brake.
Botanical name	*Pteris ensiformis 'Victoriae'.*
Interesting facts	From the Greek *pteron*, a wing.
Origin	Eastern Asia to Australia.
Position	Shade.
Temperature	Minimum winter temperature of 50F.
Watering	Never allow compost to dry out, but it should not become soggy in winter.
Feeding	Every 2 weeks throughout the growing season with a nitrogen-rich houseplant fertilizer.
Humidity	Stand the plant on a damp gravel tray and mist the leaves frequently.
Re-potting	In the spring when necessary.
Propagation	Division or from spores.

Common names	Devil's ivy, Golden pathos, Tar vine.
Botanical name	*Scindapsus aureus, Rhaphidophora aurea, Epipremnum aureum.*
Interesting facts	*Scindapsus* is the ancient Greek name for a plant looking like an ivy.
Origin	Solomon Islands.
Position	Shade.
Temperature	Minimum winter temperature of 50F.
Watering	Water well during the growing season but allow the compost to dry out between waterings in the winter.
Feeding	Every 2 weeks throughout the growing season with a nitrogen-rich houseplant fertilizer.
Humidity	Stand the plant on a damp gravel tray and mist the leaves frequently.
Re-potting	When necessary in the spring.
Propagation	Stem cuttings in the spring or summer.

Common name	Devil's ivy.
Botanical name	*Scindapsus aureus* 'Marble Queen'.
Interesting facts	See *S. aureus.*, p130
Origin	Garden origin.
Position	Shade.
Temperature	Minimum winter temperature of 50F.
Watering	See *S. aureus.*
Feeding	Every 2 weeks throughout the growing season with a nitrogen-rich houseplant fertilizer.
Humidity	Stand the plant on a damp gravel tray and mist the leaves frequently.
Re-potting	When necessary in the spring.
Propagation	Stem cuttings in the spring or summer.

Common name	Creeping moss.
Botanical name	*Selaginella.*
Interesting facts	Name derived from Latin *selago,* the name for the common or club moss of the northern temperate zone.
Origin	Mainly tropical.
Position	Shade.
Temperature	Minimum winter temperature of 55F.
Watering	Keep compost moist throughout the growing season, reduce the amount of water in winter and allow compost surface to dry out between winter waterings.
Feeding	Every 2 weeks throughout the growing season with a nitrogen-rich houseplant fertilizer.
Humidity	Stand the plant on a damp gravel tray and mist the leaves frequently.
Re-potting	When necessary in the spring.
Propagation	Stem cuttings in the spring.

GLOSSARY

TERMS

Anther Pollen bearing part of a stamen
Annual A plant which germinates, flowers and sets seed in one growing season
Corolla tube A collective term for the petals forming a tube
Hybrid A plant originating by the fertilization of one species by another. The sign X between a plant name depicts that the plant is a hybrid
Offsets Short lateral shoots bearing close rosettes of leaves, which are capable of taking root and being separated from the mother plant
Plantlet Young plant, quite often produced at the end of a long stem, can be rooted
Pot-bound Is the situation when the roots of a plant are coming out from the drainage holes and have started to curl around the inside of the pot
Rhizome A more or less swollen stem, wholly or partially underground
Stamens Male pollen-bearing part of the flower
Spores Minute reproductive body of a non-flowering plant
Stolons Creeping stems which often form new plants on it above ground level
Suckers A shoot arising adventurously from a root of a plant often at some distance from the main stem
Tuber Swollen, underground part of stem or root

TECHNIQUES

Air-layering A slanting cut is made into the stem of the plant near the growing point. This is then surrounded with moss and covered with plastic. Rooting then takes place into the moss and the rooted portion is then detached
Division The operation which involves separating a plant up into smaller sections. With houseplants this is normally done with the hands

Layering Long stems are bent down into the soil to form a 'U' shape. The base of the 'U' is cut partly through. From this region roots appear

Leaf-bud cuttings Cuttings which consist of a leaf, its axillary bud and a portion of stem

Leaf-section cuttings Cuttings which consist of a leaf or portion of the leaf excluding the axillary bud or portion of stem

Re-pot (repotting) To transfer a plant from one plant pot into another either of the same size or one slightly larger which contains fresh compost

Softwood cuttings (stem tip cuttings) Cuttings which are prepared from a young shoot which is still extending

Stem cutting (stem section cutting) The cutting up of portions of the stem which then become cuttings inserted into compost

Pegging down plantlets This involves the use of a piece of wire bent to form a 'U' shaped pin which is then turned upside down and positioned over the stem with the plantlet on the end, into cutting compost until the plantlet is rooted. Once rooted the pin and parent plant's stem are removed leaving a newly rooted plant

INDEX OF COMMON NAMES

African lilies 9
African violet 82
Allamanda 79
Aluminium plant 127
Amaryllis 30
Angels' trumpet 71
Angel's wings 120
Arrowhead vine 112
Arum lily 45
Asparagus 89
Aztec lily 42
Baby's tears 55
Banana 35
Banana passion fruits 37
Bead plant 104
Beefsteak plant 56
Begonia 12,90
Belladonna lily 10
Bell flower 18
Bird of paradise flower 85
Bird's nest fern 118
Black-eyed Susan 44
Blood lily 26
Blue Cape 39
Boston fern 125
Bottlebrush plant 17
Bromeliad 58
Bush violet 15
Busy lizzie 76
Butterfly flower 40
Camellia 67
Cape cowslip 34
Cape leadwort 39
Cape primrose 43
Castor oil plant 59
Century plant 48
Ceriman 103
Cestrum 68
Cherry pie 27
Chilean bell flower 78
Chinese evergreen 88

Chinese jasmine 31
Christmas cactus 83
Cineraria 41
Climbing Fig 101
Coral berry 63
Creeping fig 101
Creeping moss 132
Crown of thorns 23
Cupid's bower 8
Cyclamen 70
Delta maidenhead fern 116
Devil's ivy 130,131
Dumb cane 121,122
Fairy primrose 81
False aralia 93
False castor oil plant 96
False palm 94
Fan begonia 119
Fig tree 100
Finger aralia 93
Firecracker flower 22
Flame nettle 51
Flaming katy 32
Florist's chrysanthemum 19
Florists' cyclamen 70
Freckle face 55
Fuchsia 25
Geranium 38
Glory pea 20
Golden ball 53
Golden barrel 53
Golden pathos 130
Goldfish plant 69
Goosefoot plant 112
Grape ivy 107
Guinea gold vine 28
Heart leaf 126
Heliotrope 27
Herringbone plant 102
Hot water plant 8
Humble plant 57
Hydrangea 75
Iron cross begonia 50

Italian bellflower 18
Ivy 124
Jacobean lily 42
Jade plant 52
Kaffir lily 21
Kahili ginger 74
Kalanchoe 33
Koka beak 20
Lantana 77
Lobster claw 20
Mageuy 48
Maidenhead fern 116
Marmalade bush 86
Mexican bread fruit 103
Mother-in-law's tongue 108
Mother of thousands 109
Nerve plant 123
Oleander 36
Orchid 65
Painted leaf 119
Painted net leaf 123
Painted nettle 51
Painter's palette 117
Paper flower 14
Parrot's bill 20
Passion flower 37
Peace lily 84
Peristrophe 80
Persian violet 73
Pick-a-back plant 113
Piggyback plant 113
Pineapple 49
Pineapple flower 73
Pink jasmine 31
Plume asparagus 89
Pocket book plant 16
Poinsettia 24
Polka dot plant 55
Poor man's orchid 40
Pot mum 19
Purple passion vine 54
Purple velvet plant 54
Radermachera 106

Red Cape 26
Ribbon plant 95
Rose-bay 36
Rose of China 29
Rubber plant 99
Saint Bernard's lily 91
Sensitive plant 57
Shrimp plant 13
Silver vase 62
Slipper flower 16
Snake plant 108
Snake vine 28
Song of India 105
Spiceberry 63
Spider plant 91
Split leaf philodendron 103
Star of Bethlehem 18
Staghorn fern 128
Strawberry geranium 109
Stromanthe 110
Sweetheart plant 126
Swiss cheese plant 103
Sword brake 129
Syngonium 111
Tailflower 117
Tar vine 130
Ti tree 92
Touch-me-not 57
Trailing begonia 64
Urn plant 62
Variegated weeping fig 98
Vase plant 62
Wax begonia 11
Weeping fig 98
White sails 84
Yesterday, today and tomorrow 66

INDEX OF BOTANICAL NAMES

Achimenes 'Rosy Red' 8
Adiantum aemulum 116
Adiantum cuneatum 116
Adiatum raddianum 116
Aechmea fasciata 62
Agapanthus 9
Agave americana medio-picta 48
Aglanonena 'Silver Queen' *88*
Amaryllis belladonna *10*
Amaryllis formorsissima *42*
Ananas comosus variegatus 49
Anthericum comosus 91
Anthurium andreanum 117
Aralia elegantissima 93
Aralia japonica 96
Aralia sieboldii 96
Ardisia crispa 63
Aregelia marechalii 58
Asparagus densiflorus 89
Asparagus meyeri 89
Asplenium nidus 118
Asplenium nidus-avis 118
Begonia carribean Hybrid 90
Begonia masoniana 50
Begonia rex 119
Begonia semperflorens 11
Begonia sutherlandii 64
Begonia tuberhybrida 12
Beleperone guttata 13
Bougainvillea x buttiana 'Brilliant' 14
Brassia brachiata *65*
Brassia verrucosa *65*
Browallia speciosa 'Blue Troll' 15
Brunsfelsia latifolia 66
Bryophyllum uniflorum 33
Caladium hurtulanum 'Frieda Hemple' 120
Calanthea amabilis 110
Calceolaria x herbeohybrida 16
Callistemon citrinus 17
Camellia 'Inspiration' *67*
Campanula isophylla *18*

Cestrum elegans 68
Cestrum purpureum 68
Chlorophytum comosus variegatum 91
Chrysanthemum morifolium 19
Clianthus puniceus 'Albus' 20
Clivia miniata 21
Coleus blumei 51
Columnea gloriosa 69
Cordyline terminalis 'Kiwi' 92
Crassula argentea 52
Crassula portulacea 52
Crossandra infundibuliformis 22
Crossandra undulifolia 22
Cyclamen persicum 70
Datura x candida 'Plena' 71
Dieffenbachia maculata 121
Dieffenbachia picta 122
Dieffenbachia picta 'Camilla' 121
Dipladenia sanderi 79
Dizygotheca elegantissima 93
Dracaena dermensis Yellow 94
Dracaena reflexa 105
Dracaena sanderiana 95
Echinocactus grusonii 53
Epipoemnum aureum 130
Eucomis comosa 72
Eucomis punctata 72
Euphorbia milii splendens 23
Euphorbia pulcherrima 24
Exacum affine 73
Fatsia japonica 96
Fatsia japonica Gold 97
Ficus benjamina 98
Ficus elastica 'Belga' 100
Ficus pumila 101
Fittonia verschaffeltii Red and Silver 123
Franciscea latifolia 66
Fuchsia triphylla 'Gartenmeister Bonstedt' 25
Gynura Sarmentusa 54
Heamanthus natalensis 26
Hedera helix 124
Hedychium gardnerianum 74
Heliotropium arborescens 27

Heliotropium peruvianum *27*
Hibbertia scandens *28*
Hibiscus rosa-sinensis *29*
Hippeastrum hybrida *30*
Hydrangea hortensis *75*
Hydrangea macrophylla *75*
Hypoestes phyllostachya *55*
Impatiens 'New Guinea Hybrids' 76
Iresine herbstii *56*
Jasminum polyanthum *31*
Kalanchoe blossfeldiana *32*
Kalanchoe uniflora *33*
Lachanalia aloides *34*
Lachanalia tricolor *34*
Lanata montevidensis *77*
Lanata sellowiana *77*
Lapageria rosea *78*
Mandevilla splendens *79*
Maranta amabilis 110
Maranta leuconeura erythrophylla 102
Maranta 'Tricolor' *102*
Mimosa pudica *57*
Monstera deliciosa *103*
Musa 35
Neoregelia carolinae *58*
Nephrolepsis exaltata 'Bostoniensis' 125
Nephthytis hoffmannii 111
Nerium oleander *36*
Nertera granadensis 104
Nidularium meyendorfii 58
Passiflora exonensis 37
Pelargonium hortorum hybrid 38
Peristrophe speciosa 80
Philodendron scandens 126
Pilea cadierei 127
Platycerium alcicorne 128
Platycerium bifurcatum 128
Pleomele reflexa variegata 105
Plumbago capensis 39
Primula malacoides 81
Pteris ensiformis 'Victoriae' 129
Radermachera sinica 'Danielle' 106
Rhaphidophora aurea 130

Rhoicissus rhomboidea 107
Ricinus communis 59
Saintpaulia ionantha 82
Sansevieria trifaciata laurentii 108
Saxifraga sarmentosa 'Tricolor' 109
Saxifraga stolonifera 109
Schizanthus hybrida 40
Schlumbergia x buckleyi 83
Scindapsus aureus 130
Scindapsus aureus 'Marble Queen' 131
Selaginella 132
Senecio cruentus 41
Spathiphyllum wallisii 84
Sprekelia formosissima 42
Stereospermum sinicum 106
Strelitzia reginae 85
Streptocarpus 'Lady Strathallen' 43
Streptosolen jamesonii 86
Stromanthe amadilis 110
Syngonium hoffmannii hybrid 111
Sygonium podophyllum 112
Thunbergia alata 'Susie' 44
Tolmiea menziesii 113
Zantedeschia 'Lady Luck' 45